My Boat

For a free color catalog describing Gareth Stevens' list of high-quality books, call 1-800-542-2595 (USA) or 1-800-461-9120 (Canada). Gareth Stevens' Fax: (414) 225-0377.

Library of Congress Cataloging-in-Publication Data

Davies, Kay.
    My boat / by Kay Davies and Wendy Oldfield; photographs by Fiona Pragoff.
      p. cm. -- (First step science)
    Includes bibliographical references and index.
    ISBN 0-8368-1115-1
    1. Displacement (Ships)--Juvenile literature. 2. Stability of ships--Juvenile literature. 3. Boats and boating--Juvenile
literature. [1. Displacement (Ships) 2. Boats and boating.]
    I. Oldfield, Wendy. II. Pragoff, Fiona, ill. III. Title. IV. Series.
    VM157.D38 1994
    623.8'1--dc20   94-7108

This edition first published in 1994 by
Gareth Stevens Publishing
1555 North RiverCenter Drive, Suite 201
Milwaukee, Wisconsin 53212, USA

Series editor: Patricia Lantier-Sampon
Editorial assistants: Mary Dykstra, Diane Laska
Illustrations: Alex Ayliffe
Science consultant: Dr. Bryson Gore

Printed in the United States of America
1 2 3 4 5 6 7 8 9 99 98 97 96 95 94

At this time, Gareth Stevens, Inc., does not use 100 percent recycled paper, although the paper used in our books does contain about 30 percent recycled fiber. This decision was made after a careful study of current recycling procedures revealed their dubious environmental benefits. We will continue to explore recycling options.

First Step Science

My Boat

by Kay Davies and Wendy Oldfield
photographs by Fiona Pragoff

Gareth Stevens Publishing
MILWAUKEE

What colors and shapes are they?

My boat is long and red.

My boat is flat at one end. . .

and pointed at
the other end.

My boat floats on water.
It does not let water in.

If I make waves, my boat
moves away from me.

If the marbles are all at
one end of my boat. . .

it sinks!

With marbles at both ends, my boat
floats low in the water.

If I add too many marbles. . . !

Tom is making
a paper boat.

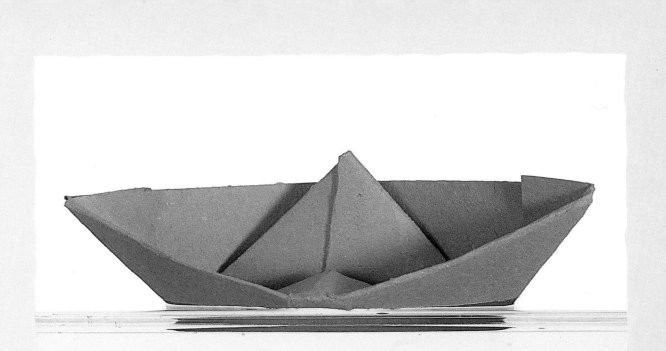

It floats on the water.

What happens when Tom's boat soaks up the water?

I'm making clay boats. Do you think they will float?

17

My clay boat has a mast and a sail.

When we blow on the sail,
my boat moves in the water.

I have made a
wooden boat.

20

With a drop of dishwashing liquid. . .

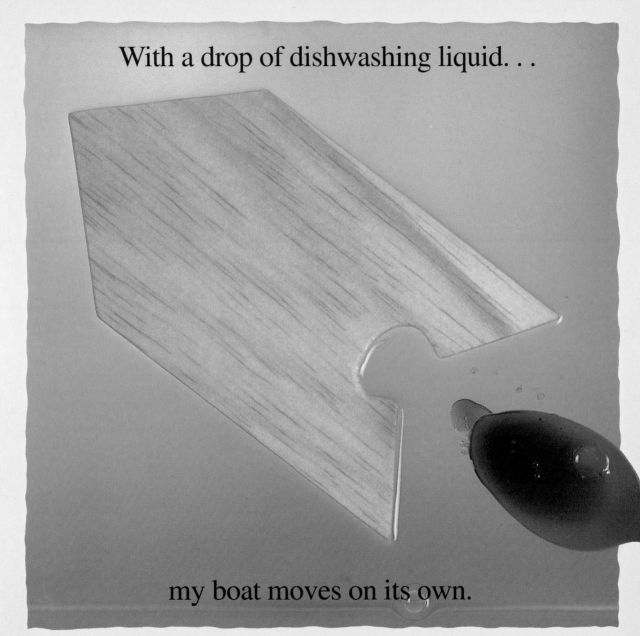

my boat moves on its own.

Under Polly's wooden boat, there is a keel.

It's hard to pull Polly's boat over.

If I tip it sideways, it
swings back up again.

We are having a race with our boats.

24

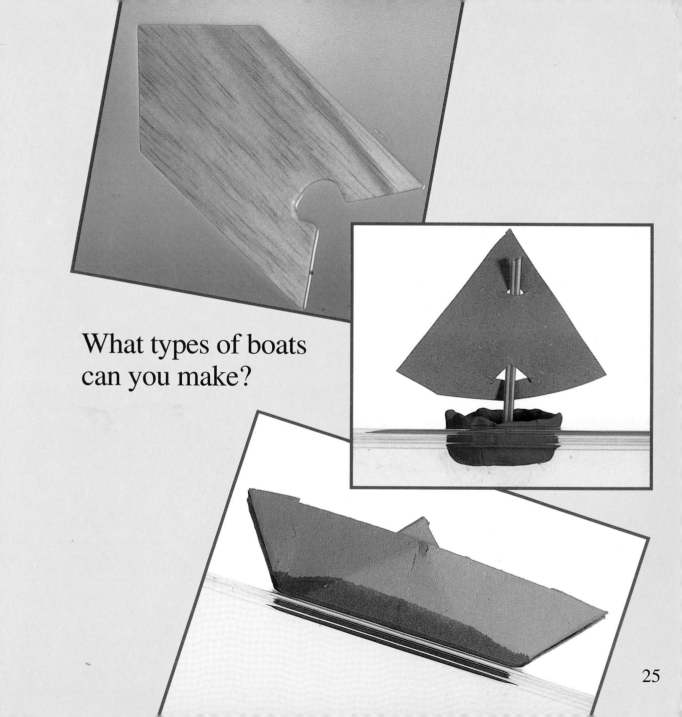

What types of boats can you make?

FOR MORE INFORMATION

Notes for Parents and Teachers

As you share this book with young readers, these notes may help you explain the scientific concepts behind the different activities.

pages 4, 5, 6, 7
Colors and shapes
Boats can be sorted into different groups according to their color or shape. The shape of a boat affects its speed in water. Most boats are pointed in the front to help them push aside the water more easily and reduce the loss of speed caused by the resistance of the water.

pages 8, 12, 15, 17
Floating boats
To make room for itself, a floating object has to push some water out of the way. This is called displacement. When an object floats, it displaces a volume of water that weighs the same as the object.

pages 9, 19, 21
Making boats move
Natural forces that push boats include waves, currents, tides, and the wind. On a sailing boat, the sails catch the wind. The angle of the sails is very important; if the wind hits the side of the sails, it makes the boat spin around.

On page 21, the dishwashing liquid reduces the surface tension of the water behind the boat. The stronger pull of the surface tension in front of the boat pulls it forward.

pages 10, 11, 12, 13
Boats and cargo

A boat can carry a heavy load if the cargo is distributed evenly. If all the cargo is at one end of the boat, the boat becomes unstable and is likely to capsize.

A ship floats at different levels depending on the weight of the cargo, the water temperature, and the amount of salt in the water. The Plimsoll line on the side of a ship indicates how low a ship can safely float in different types of water.

A boat sinks if it weighs more than the maximum amount of water it can displace.

pages 14-16
Paper boats

Paper is porous and absorbs water quickly, so a paper boat soon becomes waterlogged and sinks.

pages 17-19
Clay boats

A ball of modeling clay sinks in water, but if the same ball of clay is pressed into a boat shape, it should float.

pages 20-22
Wooden boats

Most types of wood are light enough to float on water, but they float at different levels according to their density.

The boat on these pages is made from balsa wood, a very lightweight wood that floats high in the water. A balsa wood boat will float even if it has no sides.

pages 22, 23
Keeping boats upright

A keel helps keep the center of gravity in the middle of a boat. This makes the boat more stable and less likely to capsize.

Things to Do

1. Floating and sinking

Collect some objects made from different materials, such as paper, wood, metal, or plastic. Choose objects in different shapes and sizes. Can you guess which objects will float in water? Which objects will sink? Fill a large bowl or a bathtub with water and test the objects in your collection to see if you were right. Which materials are best for making boats?

2. All sorts of boats

See if you can find out the names of different types of boats, such as trawlers, tugs, or ferries. How is the shape of each boat suited for the job it has to do? Some boats, such as the *Titanic* or the *Mary Rose*, are famous. What are the names of some other famous boats? Choose one of these boats and write a story about how it became famous.

3. Boats from nature

Try making small boats using only materials from nature, like straw or reeds. Then test your boats to see if they will float. What materials work best? Make a list of things from nature that people in different parts of the world use to make boats.

4. Boating adventure

Imagine that you live on a boat. What kind of boat is it? What supplies do you need or want to have on your boat? Where will you travel with your boat? Make or draw a miniature houseboat. Be sure to include the things you need on the boat.

Fun Facts about Boats

1. Some American Indians made canoes from the bark of birch trees. The birch bark was sewn together with thread made from tree roots. The Indians used a sticky substance called pitch to make the canoes waterproof.

2. Some people live on boats. In China, one type of houseboat is called a junk.

3. The rudder under a sailboat steers the boat. The rudder moves from side to side.

4. The body of a boat is called the hull. The front of the boat is the bow, and the rear of the boat is the stern.

5. The Inuits of Alaska and other Arctic regions use the skins from seals and walruses stretched over wooden frames to make narrow boats called kayaks and umiaks.

6. Lifeboats will not sink because of their specially crafted design. For example, if a lifeboat tips over, the weight of its engine pulls the heavier bottom back into the water so the boat is upright again.

7. Early Egyptians made boats by tying water plants called reeds together. Some people still make and use reed boats.

8. Long ago, fishing boats had eyes painted on the front, or bow. The fishermen believed the boats had spirits and that the painted eyes would help both the spirits and the fishermen find their way.

Glossary

clay — a soft type of earth that can be molded or shaped when it is wet. Clay hardens after it is exposed to heat. Clay can be used to make bricks and pottery.

flat — having a smooth, level, or even surface.

float — to rest or drift on top of a liquid or air.

keel — a piece of wood or metal on the bottom of a boat or ship.

marbles — little balls of glass used to play games.

mast — a tall pole that holds up the sails of a ship.

pointed — having a sharp tip, end, or point.

sail — a piece of strong fabric that stretches out to catch the wind and help move a boat through water.

sink — to go beneath the surface of water or some other soft substance. Boats will sink if they are loaded with too much heavy cargo or if they are not built properly.

soak — to absorb water or some other liquid.

tip — to push or knock over.

waves — ridges or swells that move across the top of a body of water.

Places to Visit

Everything we do involves some basic scientific principles. Listed below are a few museums that offer a variety of scientific information and experiences. You may also be able to locate other museums in your area. Just remember: you don't always have to visit a museum to experience the wonders of science. Science is everywhere!

Museum of Science and Industry
57th Street and Lake Shore Drive
Chicago, IL 60637

The Smithsonian Institution
1000 Jefferson Drive SW
Washington, D.C. 20560

The Exploratorium
3601 Lyon Street
San Francisco, CA 94123

Science Center of British
  Columbia
1455 Quebec Street
Vancouver, British Columbia
V6A 3Z7

Ontario Science Center
770 Don Mills Road
Don Mills, Ontario
M3C 1T3

More Books to Read

Amazing Boats
    Margarette Lincoln
    (Knopf)

Boat Book
    Gail Gibbons
    (Holiday House)

First Look at Boats
Daphne Butler
(Gareth Stevens)

Ships and Boats
Angela Royston
(Dorling Kindersley)

*Simple Science Experiments
with Water*
E. Orii and M. Orii
(Gareth Stevens)

Simple Science Projects with Water
John Williams (Gareth Stevens)

Videotapes

My First Science Video (Sony)   *Water* (Barr)

Index